ANCI

DORSET

BY ROBERT WESTWOOD

Inspiring Places Publishing
2 Down Lodge Close
Alderholt Fordingbridge
SP6 3JA

ISBN 978-0-9928073-2-0
© 2014 Robert Westwood
All rights reserved
2nd Edition
Photographs by the author except pages 13 and 18.

Contains Ordnance Survey data © Crown copyright and database right (2011)

2

Contents

Introduction

Nowhere in Dorset is far from a tangible reminder of the county's ancient past. From prehistoric causewayed camps to burial mounds, hillforts and Roman roads, Dorset is scattered with important remains that have fascinated archaeologists and delighted visitors for years.

A tour of the ancient sites of Dorset is made all the more interesting by its natural beauty. This small guide seeks to give the visitor a useful background to the ancient history of the county and to describe some of the important sites in more detail.

For convenience I have divided this period of history into the Stone Age, Bronze Age, Iron Age and Roman era. The first three are naturally characterised by the latest technology that was available, but it is not to be assumed that bronze tools and weapons were widely available in the Bronze Age. There is no sudden transition from one age to another; many ancient sites were used for hundreds of years, spanning these arbitrary and artificial divisions. The names are used for convenience and to link with other civilisations around Europe.

The Stone Age or Palaeolithic covers a huge time span starting about 500 000 years ago when humans first appeared in Britain. For thousands of years these people roamed the land hunting and gathering what food they could. They survived ice ages and interglacials using tools made of stone, bone and wood. About 15 000 years ago there came to Britain the first real modern human beings, "homo sapiens sapiens". Around this time amazing cave art was being produced in France and Spain, but none has ever been found in Britain.

From about 4000 BC things began to change dramatically. This begins the period usually referred to as the Neolithic or New Stone Age. This is when people began to domesticate animals and to grow crops; in other words, they began to farm. The earliest features we see of this time are known as causewayed camps, so called because the ditches which surround them are not continuous but crossed by causeways. There are several of these camps in Dorset.

The Bronze Age in Britain begins around 2500 BC. The first metal artefacts began to be used. Changes in burial practice are noticeable and different political and religious practices are evident. We also begin to find the remains of pottery jars or beakers, so ubiquitous that the name "beaker folk" has been used to describe the people of this age. The Bronze Age has left Dorset with hundreds of round burial barrows and the excavation of these has

told us much about this time, although the destruction of many of them in the nineteenth century has lost valuable information.

In the first millenium BC society began to change. For one thing it seems the population grew substantially and Dorset was probably one of the more densely settled areas. Around 700 BC is the commonly accepted time when the Bronze Age ended and the Iron Age began. Accompanying the change to the new material were profound social changes. A diverse and complex society emerged that has left us some spectacular remains. Things were to change again in 43 AD when the Romans arrived.

The picture shows part of the Nine Stones, a Neolithic stone circle near Winterbourne Abbas, an area rich in remains from this era and the Bronze Age.

The Stone Age

The first humans came to Britain about half a million years ago in the geological era known as the Pleistocene. This was the time of glacials and interglacials. They settled in the southern area of Britain which, although not subject to ice sheets, was much affected by the meltwaters from ice sheets to the north. They would have hunted wild animals and gathered wild plants. This simple way of life continued for thousands of years; the time between around 500 000 BP (before present) to approximately 15 000 BP is known as the Lower Palaeolithic. Many stone tools have been recovered as have the bones of wild animals such as elephants, mammoths, lions and hyenas. It is thought that humans were forced out of Britain sometime between 40 000 and 20 000 BP as the climate got colder, returning as it warned up around 15 - 13 000 BP. These migrations would not have had to cross the open sea - the English Channel was then a vast river valley fed by rivers such as the Seine, Somme and Solent.

Around fifteen thousand years ago the first real modern humans or homo sapiens sapiens appeared in Britain. We now move into the Upper Palaeolithic. For around seven thousand years they hunted on the still frozen land, wearing animal skins and using stone tools. The climate then began to warm up; the sea level rose and forests began to grow on the chalk uplands of Dorset. At about 6000 BC Britain finally became an island as the land bridge across the channel was submerged. Between about 9000 BC and 4000 BC is the time known as the Mesolithic or Middle Stone Age. It is from this age that we have the first known settlement sites in Dorset, on the Isle of Portland. At Culverwell on Portland Bill the flat bedded limestone was used to create a living floor. There is evidence of several hearths and a pit probably used for cooking. Mounds of mollusc shells have been found at a number of places along the coast; these must have formed an important part of their diet.

Traditionally the Mesolithic people have been thought of as nomadic hunter gatherers, moving from place to place to take advantage of wildlife and natural vegetation. A recent find in Northumberland, however, has led to the discovery of a Mesolithic settlement; quite a substantial round structure where wild nuts were roasted in great quantities. Carbon dating these has established that the site was inhabited for at least a hundred years, hardly a nomadic way of life. Maybe the Mesolithic folk on Portland had a similarly settled existence. There have also been Mesolithic finds near the cliffs on Dog House Hill, near Charmouth. Flint tools made around 6 - 4000 BC were found at a site that would have been at least one mile inland at the time.

Approximately six thousand years ago, around 4000 BC, the way of life which had gone on for thousands of years began to change. Rather than hunt animals, people began to keep them; they had started to farm. People learnt how to plant and reap useful plants, instead of gathering them in the wild. It is likely that these changes were initiated by immigrants from the continent. One of the results of this change of lifestyle was that, although still hard, a more efficient use of the land resulted in a growth in the population. Not only that, it meant the growth of communities facilitated by a sedentary lifestyle. This would have encouraged the building of more permanent structures across the landscape as sites for the observance of religious and social customs. Thus we begin to see monuments; burial barrows, henges, stone circles and other ceremonial features.

The earliest Neolithic structures are known as causewayed camps, hill top locations partly surrounded by ditches and crossed by "causeways". Their purpose is still open to debate, but they were probably not defensive. It seems some were visited occasionally rather than permanently inhabited: perhaps they represent a sort of transition between the nomadic way of life and a more settled existence. Others may have been permanently settled. The best known example of a causewayed camp in Dorset is at Hambledon Hill. Pottery has been found there that originated as far away as The Lizard indicating that this may have been a centre of some importance. A large cemetery has been excavated at Hambledon and this may have been its primary function. About 60 per cent of the human remains found were of children, a grim reminder of how hard life was in those times. Among the bones were also flint arrow heads, perhaps an indication that warfare was already an established feature of human existence. The function of causewayed camps is still debated, but the evidence of feasting such as the remains of animal bones and pots strongly suggests a ceremonial purpose.

Another structure that characterised the Neolithic is the long barrow, long mounds of earth which were supported by timber or large stones and which contained at one end a burial chamber. These barrows could be up to 300 feet long. We have few indications why these tombs were built and how they were used; some have argued that their alignments point to some sort of astronomical purpose. The demise of the long barrows is even more mysterious; after about a thousand years of continuous use they were apparently closed down and sealed off. At West Kennet in Wiltshire, probably the best preserved long barrow, a huge stone weighing ten tons was placed in front of the entrance and the chamber filled with earth. There is evidence that this was done over a wide area at the same time. Wor Barrow was the first excavation of General Pitt-Rivers. This long barrow near

Sixpenny Handley contained a number of burials, including a boy lying by a man with a flint arrowhead in his ribs. There were also a number of burials from Roman times, including ten that had been beheaded.

Perhaps the most mysterious Neolithic monument in Dorset is the Dorset Cursus, a seven mile long avenue of earth banks and ditches. It starts at Thickthorne Down near Cranborne and ends near the village of Pentridge. Long barrows are clustered near the ends. Its purpose is unknown, but is unlikely to have been an alien landing strip as some have suggested! Probably it too had a ceremonial function; maybe spectacular processions once wound their way along it, culminating in religious celebrations.

The picture shows one bank of the Dorset Cursus on Bottlebush Down near Cranborne. A little further south it crosses the Roman road known as Ackling Dyke. Also nearby are many Bronze Age round barrows.

Knowlton Circle

Knowlton Circle lies on the B3078 between Cranborne and Wimborne (GR SU023102). It is a unique place, with the ruins of a Norman church lying inside the well preserved bank of a Neolithic henge; clearly a place that has had religious significance for many thousands of years.

Knowlton is in fact a more complex site than it first appears. There are not one but four henges, discernible from aerial photographs. It is generally agreed that during the late Neolithic and early Bronze Age it was one of the most important ceremonial sites in Wessex, ranking in importance with Stonehenge.

In the Bronze Age Knowlton became a centre for the building of round barrows. The largest round barrow in Dorset, the "Great Barrow" can be seen 200 feet east of the circle. It is now covered by trees. Many other round barrows lie nearby.

Knowlton was once a thriving village, the centre of a Saxon hundred. Meetings of local hundreds gathered in the henge and later fairs were also held there. The village was devastated by the Black Death around 1485 and in the eighteenth century the church fell into disrepair.

Many people today still regard it as a sacred site. There is no doubt that it is a place with a very special atmosphere.

Other Neolithic Sites in Dorset

We have seen how the construction of causewayed camps and other monuments was linked to the development of fixed agricultural practices and settled communities. From around 3000 BC henges and stone circles began to appear across Britain. The most impressive of Dorset's henges, Knowlton, has already been described. Some of the county's other Neolithic remains are detailed on these two pages.

Above: The Grey Mare and her Colts. This chambered long barrow just over a mile north of Abbotsbury is around twenty-four metres long and one metre high. It would originally have been bigger. Human bones and pieces of pottery were discovered when it was excavated in the early nineteenth century.

Left: The Valley of Stones is about a mile east of the Grey Mare. It is thought that frost action in glacial times broke up the brittle conglomerate which tumbled down the valley sides. It is these rocks that have been used in the nearby Neolithic sites such as the Kingston Russell Stone Circle.

Above: The Nine Stones form a small stone circle in a wooded glade by the side of the A35 just west of Winterbourne Abbas. They can be approached via a footpath from the Little Chef to the east. The stones are sarsen or flinty conglomerate formed as the end product of weathering and soil formation in tropical conditions on an ancient chalk landscape, and were available in large numbers in the nearby Valley of Stones (previous page).

Below: Another stone circle is to be found just north-west of the Grey Mare. This is the Kingston Russell Stone Circle, consisting of eighteen fallen stones. It lies at the confluence of a number of paths on a prominent ridge with extensive views.

General Augustus Pitt-Rivers

Augustus Lane Fox was born at Hope Hall, Yorkshire. After graduating from Sandhurst he joined the Grenadier Guards and began a distinguished military career during which he fought in the Crimean War and was mentioned in dispatches for bravery.

He quickly gained an interest in the development of firearms which subsequently broadened to an interest in all kinds of artefacts. He understood that one of the keys to understanding things of the past was to study implements that were currently in use. He also appreciated that classifying and cataloguing artefacts was an important means of gaining understanding.

In 1880 Lane Fox had the good fortune to inherit his great uncle's estate on the Dorset/Wiltshire border. This was the Rushmore estate and covered 27 000 acres of the beautiful Cranborne Chase. The terms of the will insisted he changed his name to that of his relative and upon retiring from the army due to ill health Lieutenant General Augustus Pitt-Rivers devoted himself to the meticulous excavation of the numerous ancient and historic sites on the estate, including many Bronze Age round barrows. The fact that Cranborne Chase had been a royal hunting ground meant that the antiquities were better preserved there than in other parts of the country.

He is widely regarded as the father of modern archaeology and kept detailed records of all the finds on the sites he excavated. He published his findings in a lavish four volume work "Excavations in Cranborne Chase" and displayed his collections of artefacts in local museums. He once said that the recording of an excavation took about five times as long as the actual digging.

Shortly after inheriting the Rushmore estate he created the Larmer Tree Gardens (right). This was, and still is, an exotic mix of the intimate and the majestic, complete with ornate follies. It was created for the recreation of estate workers and local people; entrance was free and in 1899 there were 44 000 visitors. It remains an enchanting way to spend a Sunday afternoon.

General Augustus Pitt-Rivers, © Salisbury and South Wiltshire Museum

The Bronze Age

It is generally accepted that the Bronze Age begins around 2500 BC, but this is an entirely arbitrary division. No sudden move towards the use of bronze tools and weapons is discernible, rather a very gradual transition in which bronze artefacts become more common. It is cultural changes that really provide the distinction between the Stone Age and the first metal users. Burial in round barrows replaced long barrows and there are many examples of these in Dorset. The largest in the county is the Great Barrow at Knowlton (above), originally surrounded by a pair of concentric ditches.

We have seen that burial in round barrows replaced long barrows, and many of the ceremonial sites, the henges and stone circles, continued to be used and were developed further. Who were the people responsible for these changes and did they usurp, perhaps by violent means, the previous inhabitants?

The first round barrow burials contained "beakers", large bell-shaped clay pots. This has led to these Bronze Age inhabitants to be known as the "beaker people". Because the beakers were first made in the Rhineland it has been assumed that the beaker people were immigrants, possibly invaders. However, it may simply be that the beakers arrived by trade, a new fad on the continent that caught on over here!

Hundreds of round barrow remains are scattered all over Dorset; clearly this was a major population centre of the Bronze Age. Round barrows were typically stone chambers which were then covered over by earth. For hundreds of years they were left untouched, until in the nineteenth century it was discovered that some contained interesting artefacts. Along with the beakers and bronze daggers, a few, presumably the resting places of chieftains, contained items made of gold.

Once this was well known, landowners began to excavate the barrows in search of treasure. Since the barrows are an important means of finding out about the Bronze Age and these excavations were not carried out with any thought given to systematic collecting, we have lost a vast store of information. Luckily some landowners were responsible and put their finds on display, others buried what they didn't want and melted the gold down.

In particular we are indebted to the Victorian landowner Augustus Pitt-Rivers for his interest in the past and his determination to ensure that all archaeological sites on his vast estate were excavated in a meticulous manner and the remains preserved for posterity.

The Bronze Age spans a huge period of time from around 2500 BC to 700 - 800 BC. During all of this time the inhabitants of Britain continued to bury their dead in round barrows. Often they were built on or near Neolithic sites and many were in use for hundreds of years. There are perhaps around 2000 of them all over Dorset, but concentrated on the chalk uplands. Although the details of the burials changed over the years, the central principle remained the same, a round mound of earth over a burial or cremation. Towards the end of the Bronze Age some of the mounds contained up to a hundred pots of ashes, while at others, burials were made around the original barrow.

What was life like for these Bronze Age "beaker folk"? In Dorset the most obvious sources of information are the remains of the barrows, although excavations such as those at Bestwall, Wareham (see page 18) have added much to our knowledge. There are rare remains elsewhere in the country of Bronze Age communities. One such place is the Bronze Age "village" of Grimspound on Dartmoor. Remember that during this time the climate was considerably warmer than it is now. Consequently, people were able to live on upland regions which are much less hospitable today. Grimspound was thought to have been built around the middle of the Bronze Age and consists of a circular stone outer wall with groups of circular stone huts within. It is not known what roof materials were used. Some of the huts were lived in while others were probably used to store produce or shelter animals. If the outer wall was built for protection it is likely to have been against wolves and bears.

Maybe similar communities were scattered on the chalk upland of Dorset; if so hundreds of years of cultivation have removed the traces. Grimspound survives because climate changes rendered Dartmoor unsuitable for cultivation.

Above: Grimspound on Dartmoor is a small, walled enclosure with a number of stone huts. Bronze Age people lived in these simple dwellings over three thousand years ago when the climate was considerably warmer than it is today.

Above: Bronkham Hill on the South Dorset Ridgeway near Portesham has a remakable number of round barrows. This must have been an important site in the Bronze Age. The barrow on the right has been cut by a large excavation trench, probably in the nineteenth century.

Some of the Dorset barrows contained very rich objects, including ones made of gold as well as bronze. Unfortunately, as we have seen, many artefacts were lost to treasure hunters in the nineteenth century. There has been speculation that these were burials of important individuals, perhaps tribal chiefs, maybe even some of those behind the construction of the great henge monuments. There certainly seems to have been a well organised hierarchy of some sort to enable such huge public works to be carried out, but no one is certain whether it was armies of slaves, or workers who were willing participants in the fervour which inspired the constructions.

No other Bronze Age burials are found except those associated with barrows. It is unclear whether all people were buried in these or whether they were just reserved for those considered more important. Although many still remain, many more have been lost to the plough over the centuries.

Bronze Age Finds in Dorset

Much work has been done investigating Bronze Age sites in Dorset and the County Museum in Dorchester has a wonderful collection of artefacts. The three examples of sites detailed on these two pages present three interesting and varied windows on life in this mysterious time.

Bestwall Quarry, Wareham

The gravel extraction site at Bestwall Quarry, Wareham was excavated between 1992 and 2005. Enormous quantities of flint tools were discovered, around forty-four thousand pieces, from the late Neolithic to early Bronze Age when the land was being cleared for agriculture. A number of Bronze Age houses were excavated and the remains indicated a small, self-sufficient community. Cattle and sheep were kept and flint scrapers and awls provided evidence of leather working. Spindles and loom weights made of Kimmeridge shale also showed that wool was spun and woven. Pottery was made here throughout the Bronze Age and a large collection has been gathered. This remarkable undertaking was led by local historian Lilian Ladle and has contributed hugely to the study of life in the Bronze Age. Finds from the excavations can be viewed at the Dorset County Museum in Dorchester.

Above: The beautiful gold lozenge discovered in Clandon Barrow by Edward Cunnington. Right: One of the bronze axe heads from the Purbeck hoard. Photos courtesy of Dorset County Museum.

Above: Clandon Barrow at Martinstown near Maiden Castle.

Clandon Barrow

Clandon Barrow near Dorchester is a large bowl barrow, prominently sited on the Chalk ridge. It measures around thirty metres in diameter and is about three metres high. It was once surrounded by a ditch three metres wide. The barrow was excavated in 1882 by Edward Cunnington who found, along with a cremation urn, a copper dagger, shale mace head and a gold lozenge, similar to the one found at Bush Barrow near Stonehenge. These grave goods were thought to indicate the burial of a local chief and to be representative of a fairly widespread "Wessex Culture". More recently, examination of the artefacts has revealed extensive maritime links with other lands and it may be that they stand as a record of travels and exploits in foreign lands. This may have been very important to the local community.

Bronze Axe hoard, Isle of Purbeck

In 2007 on the Isle of Purbeck a local man with a metal detector discovered a hoard of bronze axes. Dating from around 700 BC, in the late Bronze Age, there were hundreds of the bronze axe heads, one of the largest finds ever made in Britain. Strangely, the axes were completely impractical – they were found to contain a high proportion of tin or lead, rendering them far too brittle to be used as tools, but making them more shiny. Such axes may have been used as a form of currency and they may have been some sort of ritual offering.

The Iron Age

Towards the end of the Bronze Age the landscape began to change. Increasingly we see evidence of the cultivation of the land. It seems that the main concern of society had shifted from the construction of huge ritual sites to organising and managing the land. We find coaxial (arranged in grids) field systems that derive from this time; the so called "Celtic fields". The climate was beginning to change and some upland areas were no longer as hospitable as before.

The period around 800BC was one of rapid social change. There is evidence of much trade with the continent and the introduction of new implements and weapons. Iron was being used more and more.

Did these changes take place as a result of increased communication with the continent or were they the result of a mass immigration or even invasion by people from the continent? Historians have debated this for many years, but evidence does show that Britain was at this time an integral part of a western European trade and exchange zone, with goods being transported across the North Sea, the Irish Sea and via the Atlantic as far south as Gibraltar.

Gradually the Celtic language became common and different tribes established themselves in different areas. They began to build the features which we associate with this era, the hillforts. These are found all over Britain, but nowhere are they more common than in Wessex. Dorset at this time must have been quite densely inhabited, with the land divided up in an effort to maximise production.

The earliest hillforts were built around 600 BC. They were simple affairs usually with a single bank and ditch following the contours of a hill. Some of them have remained unploughed for centuries and excavations at these, for example at Chalbury near Weymouth, reveal evidence of small round huts built on terraces and a variety of utensils and pottery used in everyday life. Large jars for storing grain were common and fine tableware indicates that life was not all hard toil.

Why were the hillforts built? Clearly their purpose was defensive; they provided shelter for whole communities and their animals. Perhaps as the population grew, thanks to more intensive farming and the organisation of the land, so competition for land grew and disputes between tribes or individual settlements increased. Towards the end of the first millenium BC the hillforts became increasingly complex, with three or even four sets of ramparts and ditches and maze like entrances. Whether this is evidence

Eggardon hillfort in West Dorset.

of more intensive inter-tribal conflict or not is open to question. Some scholars think it merely demonstrates the increasing vanity of chieftains who strove to demonstrate their power and wealth. Topped by wooden pallisades and with skilled slingers to defend them, the banks and ditches might have proved formidable obstacles to opposing tribesmen, but when the Romans arrived with their more sophisticated siege weapons and tactics, the inhabitants of Iron Age Dorset must have felt the enormous effort to build the hillforts wasted!

The people of Iron Age Dorset did not all live in hillforts; remains of Iron Age field systems are to be found all over the county. All the known Iron Age villages in Dorset are on high ground with their fields extending down from the village towards the valley bottom. However, excavations around Maiden Castle have shown that during the Middle Iron Age (300-100 BC) the area immediately around the hillfort was not occupied suggesting that the populace was concentrated within the defences. Perhaps an urban centre was developing?

The Durotriges

It has been traditionally assumed that Iron Age Dorset was part of the territory of a tribe known as the Durotriges, a name given to us by the Roman geographer Ptolemy. However, no recognisable tribal centre has ever been found, instead their supposed region is characterised by an unusually dense concentration of imposing hillforts. Martin Papworth, an archaeologist with the National Trust, has suggested that, based on settlement patterns and burial practices, Dorset was occupied by a number of diverse and distinct groups. It has been suggested that this lack of unity was unusual among other British tribes although it may be that towards the end of the Iron Age smaller groups possibly banded together into some sort of alliance and that they may have regarded themselves as "Durotriges".

There is evidence that the Durotrigan zone was a successful trading community. Ships brought varied goods to Poole Harbour and Hengistbury Head, and rivers like the Frome, Stour and Piddle became important trading routeways. A strong indication of a unified trading block is given by the widespread distribution of Durotrigan coins.

Left: Kimmeridge on the Isle of Purbeck was a major industrial centre during the Iron Age and Roman times. Jewellery was made from the hard , black bands of shale rich in organic matter, that collected in the oxygen poor seas of the Jurassic Period.

Left: Poole harbour at Lake. This site became an important port later in the Iron Age as the rising sea level made the ones on the south side of Poole Harbour more difficult to use. The Romans established their port here shortly after the invasion.

Iron Age Sites in Dorset

Many Iron Age sites have been identified throughout Dorset, and the Isle of Purbeck in particular seems to have been a major industrial and population centre during this period. Bounded by the sea to the south and east and barren heathland to the north, Purbeck was an "island" of prosperity. Rich agricultural land lies to the south of the Chalk ridge and there is evidence of Iron Age settlements along the spring line on the south side of the ridge. Salt from seawater was produced at a number of places and hard shale bands in the Kimmeridge Clay known as "blackstone" were used to make jewellery and ornaments. When polished this resembles jet and bracelets were made on lathes using flint and chert found locally as cutting tools. The round, discarded centres of this process were once common on the beach. The industry continued after the Roman conquest. Tertiary clays north of the Chalk were the basis for a thriving pottery industry. The Purbeck limestone provided another raw material for industry and, although not as ubiquitous as remains from the shale workings, broken limestone mortaria (vessels for grinding) are quite common.

Late in the Iron Age a major industrial and trading centre developed at Norden, north of Corfe Castle. A range of goods were produced here including pottery, chalk tessarae, shale goods and items of Purbeck limestone. Testament to its importance is the finding of three Roman villas nearby.

Unsurprisingly, Poole Harbour played an important part in Dorset's Iron Age commerce. Two stone structures, thought to be causeways, have been discovered projecting from Cleavel Point on the south side of Poole Harbour and nearby Green Island. They were probably harbour piers and timbers recovered from the sites have been dated to around 300 BC. This makes them part of the oldest constructed port in north west Europe. In 1964 an Iron Age log boat was discovered by dredgers working in the harbour. It, too, dated from around 300 BC, was ten metres long and is estimated to have been capable of carrying eighteen people. Too unstable for the open sea it may have been used to ferry people and goods around the harbour. It is now on display in Poole Museum.

There is much evidence of Iron Age occupation around Hamworthy on the north side of Poole Harbour. It has been speculated that rising sea level rendered the piers on the south side of the harbour difficult to use and that Hamworthy became more important. Salt was produced here and it was probably a centre for the importing of pottery. It was here that the Romans established their port during the conquest of South West England.

Dorset's hillforts - *There are too many of these to provide a complete account, but below are detailed some of the most well-known.*

Badbury Rings, north-west of Wimborne, occupied a very important strategic position. At this time Poole Harbour was surrounded to the north and west by extensive heathland which gave way quite abruptly to the rich agricultural land of the valleys of rivers like the Stour, Frome and Piddle. Badbury was situated at this junction and also in a position to protect the important routeway of the Stour. A short distance from their landing base at Hamworthy, this may have been the first hillfort of the Durotriges that the Romans encountered. It would have made great sense for Badbury to be well defended. Archaeologists have uncovered little evidence of a battle but there have been tantalising finds of

several ballista (catapult) bolts and and a javelin head. Perhaps this was the site of a battle as Vespasian led the II Augusta legion through South West England.

Hambledon and Hod Hill

Surely one of the most beautiful and atmospheric hillforts in the whole of England, Hambledon Hill overlooks the tranquil valley of the River Stour. It has fascinated archaeologists for a long time and has evidence of occupation covering thousands of years.

The earliest human structures on Hambledon are remains of a large Neolithic causeway camp on the summit plateau. Contemporary with this was a large fortified barrier on the eastern spur. Archaeologists have long debated whether causewayed camps were fortified as they do not seem to have been permanently occupied, but here there is evidence of some fortification.

Clinging to the contours of the northern spur of the hill are the ramparts and ditches of the Iron Age hillfort. Go when the sun is low in the west and you will be rewarded with a truly spectacular view. In all about 24 acres are enclosed and the ground is covered by platforms on which the Iron Age inhabitants built their huts.

Above: The western face of Hambledon Hill is the place to be as the sun sets.

Hambledon enjoyed a brief period of notoriety during the Civil War when the last stand of the "Dorset Clubmen", a group of locals who were heartily sick of the conflict and challenged all combatants, took place on the hill. They were rounded up without too much bloodshed by Cromwell's men and locked in the local church for the night. They were released in the morning after a stern lecture by the future Lord Protector.

Hod Hill is separated from its neighbour Hambledon Hill by a small valley. Another Iron Age hillfort, it is puzzling why they were built so close together. Perhaps it was an overspill town? Hod Hill is unusual in that it was used by the Romans, as most hillforts were abandoned after the conquest. The Roman army built a fort in the north-west corner of the hill; aerial photographs show this clearly. Walk round the ramparts and enjoy the spectacular views, and in Spring a profusion of wild flowers.

As might be expected, Hod Hill fell quickly to the Roman legion. Excavations have enabled us to piece together this interesting episode. Just prior to the Roman invasion occupation on the hill seems to have undergone a rapid expansion. There is evidence that the entire area was covered with huts. At the largest hut a collection of Roman ballista bolts was found. Apparently, aware that this was the chieftain's house, the Romans subjected it to a barrage of catapult bolts, killing him almost immediately. The rest of the inhabitants quickly surrendered.

Maiden Castle

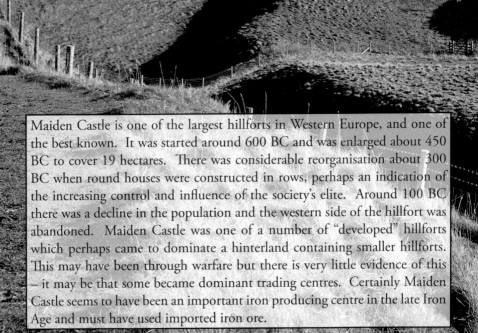

Maiden Castle is one of the largest hillforts in Western Europe, and one of the best known. It was started around 600 BC and was enlarged about 450 BC to cover 19 hectares. There was considerable reorganisation about 300 BC when round houses were constructed in rows, perhaps an indication of the increasing control and influence of the society's elite. Around 100 BC there was a decline in the population and the western side of the hillfort was abandoned. Maiden Castle was one of a number of "developed" hillforts which perhaps came to dominate a hinterland containing smaller hillforts. This may have been through warfare but there is very little evidence of this – it may be that some became dominant trading centres. Certainly Maiden Castle seems to have been an important iron producing centre in the late Iron Age and must have used imported iron ore.

Maiden Castle was famously excavated in the 1930s by Sir Mortimer Wheeler. His discovery of a cemetery at the eastern entrance with a number of mutilated bodies, including one with a Roman ballista bolt embedded in its spine (this fascinating find is on display in the Dorset County Museum in Dorchester), led him to propose that here was evidence of a defining battle during the Roman conquest. However, of the fifty-two bodies uncovered, only fourteen showed signs of mutilation and it may be that these were brought here, possibly after a battle elsewhere. Certainly the body with the catapult bolt in the spine seems to indicate an armed conflict somewhere. So, the popular conception of the siege of Maiden Castle, with the Roman legion under the command of the future emperor Vespasian, may not represent what actually happened.

Hengistbury Head

Hengistbury Head on the south side of Christchurch Harbour has provided evidence of occupation from around 10 000 BC to the end of the Roman era. In the Upper Palaeolithic or Old Stone Age, hunter gatherers would have spread northwards from Europe as the ice retreated. With no English Channel to impede them Hengistbury would have presented as a prominent hill overlooking a wide river valley to the south. Tools and pottery finds from the Mesolithic suggest a substantial occupation of the headland. Towards the end of the Neolithic and the beginning of the Bronze Age Hengistbury came to be used as a place of burial and perhaps of ritual.

In the Iron Age this area became a site of great importance. As iron working developed and skills were exported from the continent, the presence of naturally occurring ironstone led to the development of iron smelting and working. Double dykes were constructed across the neck of land separating the headland from the coastal plain, presumably for defensive purposes. A busy port grew up on the northern side of the headland, importing exotic goods from the continent and exporting iron products and agricultural produce. The rivers Stour and Avon which empty into Christchurch Harbour provided valuable inland routeways.

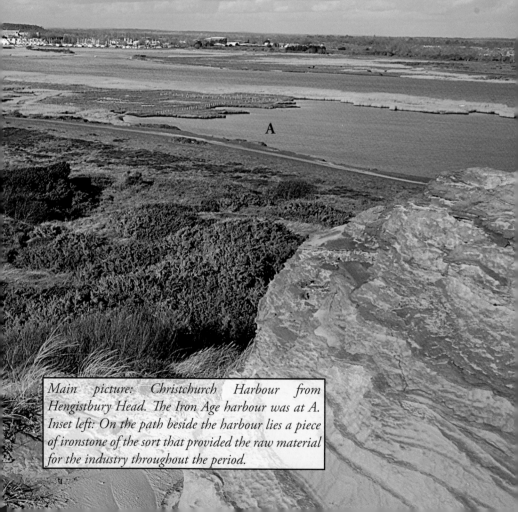

A

Main picture: Christchurch Harbour from Hengistbury Head. The Iron Age harbour was at A. Inset left: On the path beside the harbour lies a piece of ironstone of the sort that provided the raw material for the industry throughout the period.

Pilsdon Pen

Pilsdon Pen (below right) is the second highest point in Dorset after nearby Lewesdon Hill. There are magnificent views from the summit over the Marshwood Vale. Like many other hillforts Pilsdon had a long history of occupation before the Iron Age. It was abandoned after the Roman conquest.

Several other hillforts are nearby and well worth a visit. These are Lewesdon Hill, Lambert's Castle and Coney's Castle. The Monarch's Way, a long distance footpath tracing the escape of King Charles II after the Battle of Worcester, traverses the hillfort.

Poundbury (right)

A rectangular hillfort overlooking Dorchester that was, again, originally a Bronze Age enclosure. Worth visiting for the view of the Roman aqueduct (see page 33) from its northern side. In the nineteenth century Isambard Kingdom Brunel wanted to drive a new railway line through the fort but local opposition forced the construction of a tunnel instead. It was this coordinated action that led to the formation of the Dorset Archaeological Association.

Spetisbury hillfort lies between Blandford and Wimborne. In 1857 a railway cutting exposed a pit with over one hundred skeletons. Some showed signs of violence and one had a spear lodged in the skull. This was originally thought to be evidence of a battle but later examination showed the skeletons probably came from a number of different conflicts at different times.

The Romans

They came and they conquered; and it was all settled very quickly (at least as far as Dorset was concerned). Julius Caesar had been over before in 53 BC, but that was only a reconnaisance. In AD 43 they were back in force. Emperor Claudius needed a substantial conquest to boost his popularity ratings and Britain looked like a good bet. As was to be the case with Napoleon eighteen hundred years later, a large continental empire existed to back up the invading forces. Unlike in Napoleon's time, no well equipped and organised navy was available to keep the enemy away from these shores.

Aulus Plautius was in charge of the invasion, and after a relatively unopposed landing, he gave a general named Vespasian (the future emperor) command of the II Augusta legion with the mission to subdue the southern part of Britain. He proceeded quickly. Some of the tribes of the south and south-east had had contact with the Romans previously. It seems likely that some actively collaborated with them and were to do very well out of it later; witness the sumptuous palace at Fishbourne near Chichester. It was a different matter, however, when the legion came to what we now call Dorset. This was the land of the Durotriges where many strongly defended hillforts dotted the landscape.

If the Durotriges had been a well organised, coherent society they might have offered some real resistance to the Roman army. However, the many hillforts represented not a mutual defence system but a fragmented society where many local chieftains sought to further their power and standing. The Romans were able to tackle the hillforts one by one, it seems without fear of attack by their victims' neighbours. Maybe they would have done much the same had the Durotriges pulled together as the ancient Greek states did when faced by a Persian invasion, but it must be remembered that although the Romans possessed superior weapons, military technology and strategy, and were undoubtedly better trained, it was still only a single legion that was sent to conquer the south. That roughly equates to under 6000 professional legionaries plus auxillary troops.

The Romans record over twenty separate battles by Vespasian's legion, presumably many at a hillfort. It must have got easier and easier for them although some tough encounters are recorded. With such a relatively small army we must assume Roman casualties were fairly light.

How long this took is uncertain. The Romans needed time to establish a harbour at Hamworthy near Poole and to construct roads and legionary fortresses. It cannot have happened over one summer. The fact that the Durotriges continued to defend their hillforts indicates either a very belligerent attitude or a lack of any central authority. We do not know if there was a Durotrigan "king" at this time.

Once the conquest had been completed the Romans set about "Romanising" their new subjects. Perhaps local leaders were inducted into the ways of Roman life and shown the benefits of cooperation. Whatever happened, before too long the Durotriges of Dorset were no longer living in wind-swept hillforts but were enjoying luxuries like public baths at new towns such as Durnovaria (Dorchester). The more successful, or perhaps those who had cooperated earlier and more fully, were living in splendid villas with central heating and extravagant mosaics.

Left: The Roman Town House in the grounds of the County Hall is the only example of a fully exposed Roman town house in Britain. It dates from the fourth century. It was discovered in the 1930s and lies in the corner of the north and west town walls. Several burials were found associated with the site including a number of infants.

Right: A mosaic from the Roman Town House. Mosaics were often bought "off the shelf" and transported to their destination in segments. More wealthy owners could afford bespoke mosaics. Also visible in the Town House is the remains of a hypocaust system that once provided underfloor heating to part of the house.

The Romans built towns and roads and local industries grew and flourished. Remains of these have been found all over Dorset. In the Isle of Purbeck we see evidence of quarrying for stone, particularly the Portland Stone and Purbeck marble. These were used for major building works and for decorative purposes. A hard shale at Kimmeridge was extracted and carved and turned into decorative artefacts and jewellery. Roman villas have been excavated at various sites such as Dewlish near Dorchester and at Hinton St. Mary. At Dewlish we see evidence that an Iron Age farm preceded the villa; perhaps here is an example of an Iron Age farmer who grew prosperous under Roman rule. Hinton St. Mary is interesting in that a mosaic was discovered with a picture of Christ, a very early indication of the spread of Christianity to Britain.

At a site on Cranborne Chase the Channel 4 Time Team discovered remains that indicated a continuity of occupation from the Bronze Age, through the Iron Age to Roman times. Finds included a simple Iron Age burial and parts of a Roman bath house, surely indicative of a villa.

North of Dorchester at Poundbury we can see the remains of a Roman aqueduct that once brought fresh water nine miles to the people of Durnovaria. To the north they built a dam to create a lake and then constructed a clay channel with a wooden lid that followed the contours of hill sides down to the town. It was an extraordinary feat, not so much the construction, but the surveying which ensured that a gradient existed, just enough to allow the water to flow at the right rate.

Below: The Roman aqueduct near Poundbury, Dorchester.

Durnovaria grew into a sophisticated town. The usual trappings of Roman affluence have been found there such as mosaics, hypocaust (central heating) systems, bath houses and roads. At nearby Maumbury on the site of an ancient Neolithic henge complex, an amphitheatre was built capable of seating around 10 000 people. No doubt the gladiatorial spectacles proved popular here just as they did with the citizens of Rome and helped reinforce the idea that they really were better off under Roman rule.

Roman Roads in Dorset

Roman roads criss-crossed Dorset, spreading out from the important port facility at Hamworthy. An important route joined Durnovaria with Vindocladia (near Badbury), another Iron Age site that has associations with the end of the Roman Age and the adventures of the legendary Romano-British leader named Arthur.

The Ackling Dyke is a Roman road that links Badbury Rings with Old Sarum, two Iron Age hillforts that became Roman towns. It is one of the best preserved Roman roads in England and can still be walked. The best place to see it is from the B3081 at Handley Hill near Sixpenny Handley (GR SU 003136, OS sheet 184). The road can clearly be seen stretching away into the distance and it is possible to walk along it in either direction.

Above: Maumbury Rings was a Neolithic henge converted to an amphitheatre in about 100 AD by the Romans. It was only used for a short while.

Ackling Dyke is the best preserved Roman road in southern Britain. This stretch lies just north-west of Cranborne on the B3081.

Once the Romans had conquered a province the rapid construction of roads was vital to enable garrison troops to move quickly to deal with any uprisings. Naturally they were also of huge benefit to trade; none more so than the Roman road serving the harbour at Hamworthy, Poole. This great natural harbour, the world's second biggest, was an obvious place for the Romans to establish a port.

Roman roads were cleverly designed but fairly simple to execute. First two parallel ditches were dug with the excavated earth and stone being thrown into the middle to produce a raised platform known as an "agger". A shallow trench 8 – 10 feet wide was then dug in this and subsequently filled with stones to form the metalled surface of the road. The agger was lined with kerbstones to keep everything secure.

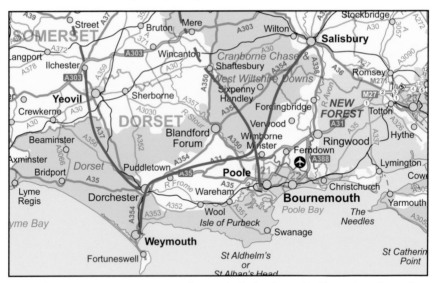

Map showing Dorset's Roman roads. Vindocladia (near Badbury Rings) north-west of Wimborne and Dorchester were the major route centres.

The End of an Era

Right on the edge of the Dorset/Hampshire border, indeed it marks the border for a number of miles, is an intriguing feature. Known as Bokerley Dyke, it is a substantial earth bank that stretches north-south across the countryside. Built in the Bronze or early Iron Age, it was re-modelled around 350AD. Originally probably a political boundary, its later purpose has been the subject of debate but it has usually been assumed to have been a defensive structure. This was the time when Rome was on the verge of pulling out of Britain, the population of southern England must have been very nervous about their future; they faced a new threat of invasion, this time from the Saxons of northern Europe.

Bokerley Dyke may have been a line of defence against the Saxon invaders. We know that shortly after 500 AD the Saxons landed at Lymington and won a battle near Southampton. The Welsh monk Gildas, writing around this time tells us of a great victory over the Saxons at "Mons Badonicus". Writing much later, the historian Nennius actually mentions a British warrior by name at the Battle of Badon, a certain Arthur.

Was Bokerley Dyke a defensive line that was overcome by the Saxons as a prelude to the famous battle at Mount Badon? Was the battle fought at Badbury Rings? Circumstantial evidence certainly fits in with these possibilities. Badbury is on a Roman road near an important crossing point of the River Stour. It is a likely place for such a battle to have been. There is also evidence that the Saxons subsequently moved north and left Dorset in peace for a while. Whatever happened, it is a fitting place to conclude our story of ancient Dorset. Perhaps thanks to the legendary Arthur, Dorset enjoyed a brief extension of the civilised way of life it had known under the Romans.

Below: Bokerley Dyke and right, the view east from the top.

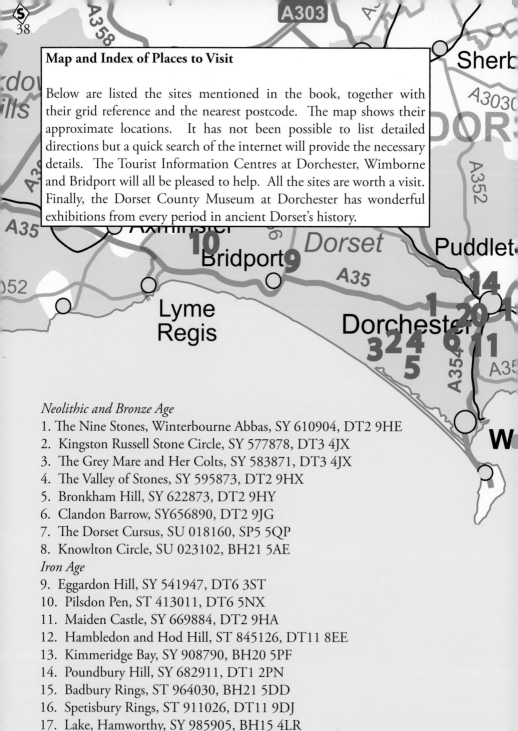

Map and Index of Places to Visit

Below are listed the sites mentioned in the book, together with their grid reference and the nearest postcode. The map shows their approximate locations. It has not been possible to list detailed directions but a quick search of the internet will provide the necessary details. The Tourist Information Centres at Dorchester, Wimborne and Bridport will all be pleased to help. All the sites are worth a visit. Finally, the Dorset County Museum at Dorchester has wonderful exhibitions from every period in ancient Dorset's history.

Neolithic and Bronze Age

1. The Nine Stones, Winterbourne Abbas, SY 610904, DT2 9HE
2. Kingston Russell Stone Circle, SY 577878, DT3 4JX
3. The Grey Mare and Her Colts, SY 583871, DT3 4JX
4. The Valley of Stones, SY 595873, DT2 9HX
5. Bronkham Hill, SY 622873, DT2 9HY
6. Clandon Barrow, SY656890, DT2 9JG
7. The Dorset Cursus, SU 018160, SP5 5QP
8. Knowlton Circle, SU 023102, BH21 5AE

Iron Age

9. Eggardon Hill, SY 541947, DT6 3ST
10. Pilsdon Pen, ST 413011, DT6 5NX
11. Maiden Castle, SY 669884, DT2 9HA
12. Hambledon and Hod Hill, ST 845126, DT11 8EE
13. Kimmeridge Bay, SY 908790, BH20 5PF
14. Poundbury Hill, SY 682911, DT1 2PN
15. Badbury Rings, ST 964030, BH21 5DD
16. Spetisbury Rings, ST 911026, DT11 9DJ
17. Lake, Hamworthy, SY 985905, BH15 4LR
18. Hengistbury Head, SZ 175905, BH6 4EW